Weekend visit.

I0478871

Author:

Women 4 Justice Publishing N.Y.C.

In association with: The T.A.N. Network,

For Civil Rights Redress, accountability,

when a child is tortured, hurt,harmed, violated

Under State Supervision . . .

#OurRightsDoMatter

Intro.

Constitutional Law . . .

shall play significant in a statewide 1st win of its kind in such tri-state (3rd district) relating to **Federal Court NJ-DE-PA, to assist other Falsely Accused Parents, grandparents** throughout our tri-state/nationwide.

CHAPTER I

Yes...I do have rights as an American...

When a child packs her Barbie pink bag, with her little sister and gets in the car, on a Friday for a weekend 4th of july visit, she is due home as in accordance with a post-divorce court order, on a Sunday by the evening hour of 7 p.m.

Not 14 days later.

A CONSTITUTIONAL RIGHT TO GO HOME …

When the author girls left for a holiday weekend visit to PGM(paternal grandmother)residence, and to see the father, she did not imagine, and no reasonable sound-minded loving parent can imagine, your child would be abducted/taken/violated for years to come. Such little girls were alert, happy,good little girls with all they ever needed, in life, at ages 10, and only 7 when such violation had arise by DCPP,DYFS,DCF employees. Their lives have forever changed years later.

This docu-series Volume 1 THROUGH 15 enumerate such fact(s) involving such sad case, and also highlights such victory that has arise out of such clear severe gruesome pain to the three [prior]victims of a cps agency who, as experts agree without warning. This…is another part of their story … A true story where you're one day playing with your little sibling hopscotch at the local nice clean parks, and or jumping rope with your sister, and peers at your elementary school and as a parent you're home baking cookies to enjoy with the kids and your family,expecting your children to come home, to where they are the most safe,(with you.) Another minute you're learning the state, and or it's individual state employees committed the ultimate crime against your child, you and your family as a whole. We thank you all for reading, and your ongoing support, and if the books being published, throughout, by Women4JusticePublishingNYC and T.A.N. for Civil Rights Redress, shall help even just 1 innocent good soul, then the author's job is done … We thank you, for reading …

THE WEEKEND VISIT …

> Entered 2 little girls good life and turned it upside down.

> Ignored the U.S.Constitution involving three American Citizens who has rights, and shall now exercise such right per liable caseworker/social worker who caused so much harm.

Weekend Visit...

A CONSTITUTIONAL RIGHT TO GO HOME ...

> Took it upon one's self to distort,circumvent and withheld such significant evidence,it shocks the conscience of all reasonable minds.

July 3rd-4th

· Visit to grandma/dad takes place approximately 12 noon.

· Two little healthy well-taken care of girls due back on Sunday.

· Caseworker on day of arrival to the grandmother's was told NOT to give the girls back to the parent, the author of such series and lawsuit winning in the U.S.District Federal Court,filed by way of pro-se.

· Caseworker took it upon herself/himself to keep girls without the necessary judicial court order/court authorization/and or a warrant to seize the children ... (Violation "1") and a significant one at that.

· During the weekend holiday visit, the girls were examined without mom knowledge, without mother's consent for days ...

. During such time, the caseworker, 1 specifically later documented such examination and the Division Youth Family Services findings...

On July 3rd throughout 10th and throughout week 2 from July 10th throughoiut the 15th/16th not one, but a multitude of employees for the state agency delineated that:

· A.) Child was fine.

B.)Both girls were examined by a "dr." earlier along with CPS.

C.)Both girls were happy.

D.)Both girls were active,alert, over PGM residence.

E.) Both girls were playing and clearly not at any risk.

A CONSTITUTIONAL RIGHT TO GO HOME …

State employee adds on how MOM is a lovely well-spoken young lady and own her 1 family nice bi-level house with a pool in back and in a great area, she reside with her daughter's then only 10 and 7.

The state employee/CPS cites clearly on the record, memorializing in a multi-page report, (internal cps files later discovered/such bombshell of factual, citing in their reports, that based on the findings by such caseworkers, the division was not able to prove abuse against such parent, let alone neglect, [end quote]

-                                    .

Such report (significant) was written clearly by DYFS,DCPP caseworker who seen the girls week of July 3rd, on the day and or week in question along with another male employee for the state and to add, "There is no legal basis, nor do the DIVISION have any legal authority to keep the girls away from their own mother." [end quote]

Worker @ DCPP adds, "I will now go and advise the grandmother the girls can go home. DYFS can't prove/can't substantiate abuse and or even neglect, of either child.

"Such report never made it to the judge's chambers."

Such government state employee official internal CPS report clearly was inextricably significant evidence, that cleared naturally the child mother and if known, as shall **support** the lawsuit filed for civil right damages, if known, would have naturally allowed 2 little girls the right to be returned, that weekend, and during such week of their unlawful and illegal, and or their unconstitutional seizure by Union County CPS.

CHAPTER II

Other winning suits involving CPS in our tri-state area, NJ,DE.PA, and nationwide related cases.

The **constitution has been completely ignored by Division Youth Family Services,New Jersey's Child Protection Agency**,whose over the past five to ten plus years, have lost multiple lawsuits (1) of the most highest paid out, that won, nationwide and in the tri-state NJ-DE-PA, was publicized and involved multiple clear error(s)leading to such liability of caseworkers, supervisors et.al, along with clear act(s) of such incompetencies by CPS employees,along with multiple lies told by a caseworker who worked for the Division Youth Family Services aka "DYFS" AKA "DCF" AKA DCPP.

To avoid a trial that would have most likely experts agree resulted in even more damage(s) **settlement of 12.5 million** where brothers were able to win,premise on starvation, wasn't properly fed by adoptive parents,physical, verbal abuse emotional abuse, and living basically in horror for some time while under the state of nj supervision of their agency now known as D.C.P.P.

Evidence also where 1 of the caseworkers assigned were altering her own file to express she was doing her job,**by'visiting"**the boys" and each visit,there were no issues with the boys.(Jackson boys)in Collingswood.

However...

(later)when it was discovered 1 of the kids were "eating out of a garbage can age 18 **malnourished** and the other brothers later bemoan of, emotional, physical abuse"and torture inside of the actual home while UNDER STATE SUPERVISION.

Author has consistently *interviewed with the acting attorney in south jersey near DE.,border who has said, how, the lawsuit involving such* **CLEAR shocking** facts,is all but won. State shall take us through the states though,simply to as lawyer(s)put it to prolong the **"inevitable."**

The constitutional rights of mom/daughter have been *violated.*

 This will ***not*** be hard to prove as case move forward and or that is clearly was not "reasonable <u>at such time of the federal violation</u>;et;al., state violation.

CHAPTER III

-CASE LAW SUPPORTIVE OF SUCH FACT-

The rights of parents <mark><u>to enjoy</u></mark> a relationship with their children is of <mark><u>constitutional dimension</u></mark>. In re Guardianship of K.H.O., 161 N.J. 337, 346 (1999) (citing Stanley v. Illinois, 405 U.S. 645, 92 S. Ct. 1208, 31 L. Ed.2d 551 (1972));

In re Adoption of Children by G.P.B., Jr., 161 N.J. 396, 403-04 (1999); New Jersey Div. of Youth and Family Servs. v. A.W., 103 N.J. 591 (1986)). Parents have a constitutionally protected, fundamental liberty interest in raising their biological children. Santosky v. Kramer, 455 U.S. 745, 753, 102 S. Ct. 1388, 1394, 71 L. Ed.2d 599, 606 (1982).

The Federal and State Constitutions protect the inviolability of the family unit. Stanley, supra, 405 U.S. at 651, 92 S. Ct. at 121-13, 31 L. Ed. 2d at 558-59; A.W., supra, 103 N.J. at 599.

DCF,DYFS,DCPP et.al, at each turn, have attempted to alter the Appeal Directives in the mother's (prior)DCF FN matter,by simply advising 4 to 5 family court judges, of how the "mental experts" professionals all agreed, mom will be a danger to the child is ever returned, premise on"1"isolated spanking at 10 years old, to daughter, leaving no serious injuries, no bruising.

The child was healthy and happy, brought up perfectly with a doting suburban mom,as her sister.

State knew this, per caseworker,but the withheld file(s)later discovered prove such knowledge/known to the state employees,ALL who are now on hook for such damages relating to the agency DYFS,DCPP,DCF.

In any event...

When CPS are assigned to a family;

The premise as to **why** the child, has been remove in the first place, has to be remedied. DYFS are not allow to just simply lie, submit false reports,withheld "real"reports"and work outside the scope of their employment, circumvent the laws here in N.J.and or ignore the policy for which allow the parent to have the chance to procure custod;and or to leave open-ended allegations of serious nature "un-investigated"to stand as the truth.

Parent has a fundamental right to nurture child/to have the child returned everyone, after and or if there is a substantiated abuse or neglect incident,

if the parent through such service(s)plan created by the caseworker,approve by "DCF supervisor" where the parent is able to effectively demonstrate,he or she is willing and clearly able to eliminate the harm that had lead to the child being detained by DYFS;and or the harm prior,that was facing the child or is and or is willing to provide a safe and stable home for the child.

This was **not** done in the author case, as media validate, in such meritorious lawsuit.

The hinderance of evidence, the neglect to adhere to multiple Appellate Decisions, the complete lack of regard for a Appellate Court, who clearly directed DYFS to investigate or return the children/and or parenting time/visitation,has cost two little girls their sanity, a safe home, loving parent,and the right to be free from neglect,abuse,harm, rape, sex abuse, bullying, medical neglect, educational neglect...

All of what has occurred only when the girls were deprive the CONSTITUTIONAL RIGHT by law,to be return;and or left alone on or about July 3rd 4th holiday weekend, several summer's ago by DCPP,DYFS,DCF.

Dispositional Review(After 1 substantiated incident)or no substantiated abuse/neglect-

CPS are by law, suppose to work with parent to have child returned,during dispositional and not use "any allegations'against the parent,if the allegations were not supported by:

- ➢ Credible, reliable, competent evidence from witness collection,physical evidence.

- ➢ In the author's case, such dispositional took place 05,but child was **not** return.

- ➢ DYFS,rather advocate for a crack-fein father,on police record for heroine in 90s to allow this troubled person,to have "full legal sole"custody.

- ➢ **Court granted such, ignoring mom completely,causing her to file another appeal.**

-Chapter III-

FIGHT HARD

The author altogether fought almost 8 years in family superior court, for what was right and going on 5 years at time of book publishing in the Federal U.S.District Court, while she has applied at multi-california law schools and also east coast, after succeeding at such level as a pro-se litigant, against state employee(s) who assumed her family would allow for no accountability to take place. CPS this time as experts agree, messed with the wrong family.

CPS has a tendency of taking clear advantage of those who are not acclimated with:

> Their constitutional rights as a family.

> Their fundamental rights as a parent.

Such rights, as an American to U.K.,child protection services employees love to ignore.

As 1 expert says to our effective network, until they are sued. And thankfully, we are seeing more of this every day per violation by a state employee.

As:

Such parent, the author, for almost a decade was deprived the fundamental right to continue to raise, nuture her own children, denied such parental rights, even though it was clear, she was more than a fit, educated astute loving good parent to her daughter's, and had no history whatsoever of drug-addiction, alcoholism, et.al, as the APPEAL (NJ highest court)even made reference to how such action(s)by the DIVISION(DCPP,DCF)had affected her parental rights. CPS employee still ignored such decision for years, in violation of such parent's right to her own girls.

CHAPTER IV

Case Law demonstrate what the author already knew.

What **any** astute mind would know exist. (***except*** CPS.)

Some additional case law(s)throughout our U.S.A., that support such importance of a sacred bond/relationship in regard to such child and (a good loving parent) as high as our Supreme Court, in which CPS continue to violate it seems, as 1 expert says, "*until* they are sued accordingly, in a timely fashion, and held accountable." We now share in our book series, some with you below, that support not only our state, but nationwide.

CPS are the only ones who do not get that you're not to violate such sacred/loving natural bond with a family. Luckily more are learning and now are seeing that you're truly able to sue a caseworker, per state employee who has clearly violated your rights …

E.G.(Example Given)

 "No case authoritative within this circuit, however, had held that the state had a comparable obligation **to protect children from their own parents**, and we now know that the obligation *__does not exist in constitutional__* law." **K.H. Through Murphy v. Morgan, 914 F.2d 846 (C.A.7 (Ill.), 1990.**

"The *right* to marry, have children and maintain relationship with children are **fundamental rights protected by the Fourteenth Amendment and thus, strict scrutiny is required of any statutes that directly and substantially impair those rights." P.O.P.S. v. Gardner, 998 F2d 764 (9th Cir. 1993)**

 "Parents right to rear children without undue governmental interference is a fundamental component of due process." Nunez by Nunez v. City of San Diego, 114 F3d 935 (9th Cir. 1997).

"*The rights* of parents to the care, custody and nurture of their children is of such character that it cannot be denied without violating those fundamental principles of liberty and justice which lie at the base of all our civil and political institutions, *and* such right is a fundamental right protected by this amendment (First) and Amendments *5, 9, and 14.*" **Doe v. Irwin, 441 F Supp 1247; U.S. D.C. of Michigan, (1985).**

The United States Supreme Court has stated:

"There is a presumption that fit parents act in their children's best interests, Parham v. J. R., 442 U. S. 584, 602; there is normally no reason or compelling interest for the State to inject itself into the private realm of the family to further question fit parents' ability to make the best decisions regarding their children." Reno v. Flores, 507 U. S. 292, 304.

"The state may <u>not</u> interfere in child rearing decisions when a fit parent is available." **Troxel v. Granville, 530 U.S. 57 (2000).**

"Even when blood relationships are strained, parents retain ***vital interest*** *in preventing* irretrievable *destruction of their family life*;

"Loss of First Amendment Freedoms, for even <mark>minimal</mark> periods of time, unquestionably constitutes irreparable injury.

Though First Amendment rights are not absolute, they may be curtailed only by <u>interests of vital</u> importance, the burden of proving which rests on their government." Elrod v. Burns, 96 S Ct 2673; 427 US 347, (1976).

Law and court procedures that are "fair on their faces" but administered "with an evil eye or a heavy hand" was discriminatory and violates the equal protection clause of the Fourteenth Amendment.

Yick Wo v. Hopkins, 118 US 356, (1886).

<u>if anything, persons faced with forced dissolution of their parental rights</u> have more critical need for procedural protections than do those resisting state intervention into ongoing family affairs." **Santosky v. Kramer, 102 S Ct 1388; 455 US 745, (1982).**

"Parents have a ==fundamental== constitutionally protected interest in continuity of legal bond with their children." **Matter of Delaney, 617 P 2d 886, Oklahoma (1980).**

"The liberty interest of the family encompasses an interest in retaining custody of one's children and, thus, a state may not interfere with a parent's custodial rights absent due process protections." **Langton v. Maloney, 527 F Supp 538, D.C. Conn. (1981).** k. "Parent's right to custody of child is a right encompassed within protection of this amendment which may not be interfered

"**Parent's** interest in custody of her children is a liberty interest which has received considerable constitutional protection; a parent who **is deprived of custody** of his or her child, even though temporarily, suffers thereby grievous loss and such loss **deserves** extensive due process protection."

In the Interest of Cooper, 621 P 2d 437; 5 Kansas App Div 2d 584, (1980).**"The Due Process Clause of the Fourteenth Amendment requires that severance in the parent-child relationship caused by the state occur only with rigorous protections for individual liberty interests at stake." Bell v. City of Milwaukee, 746 F 2d 1205; US Ct App 7th Cir WI, (1984**

"A parent's right to care and companionship of his or her children are so fundamental, as to be guaranteed protection under the First, Ninth, and Fourteenth Amendments of the United States Constitution." In re: J.S. and C., 324 A 2d 90; supra 129 NJ Super, at 489.

The Court stressed, "**the parent-child** relationship is an important interest that undeniably warrants deference and, **absent a powerful** countervailing interest, protection. **A parent's interest in the companionship, care, custody** and management of his or her children rises **to a constitutionally secured right,** given the centrality of family life as the focus for personal meaning and **responsibility." Stanley v. Illinois, 405 US 645, 651; 92 S Ct 1208, (1972**

Quilloin v. Walcott, 98 S Ct 549; 434 US 246, 255^Q56, (1978).

"The parent-child relationship is a liberty interest protected by the Due Process Clause of the 14th Amendment."

Bell v. City of Milwaukee, 746 f 2d 1205, 1242^Q45; US Ct App 7th Cir WI, (1985).

"No bond is more precious and none should be more zealously protected by the law as the bond between parent and child." Carson v. Elrod, 411 F Supp 54 645, 649; DC E.D. VA (1976).

"A parent's right to the preservation of his relationship with his child derives from the fact that the parent's achievement **of a rich and rewarding life is likely to depend significantly on his ability to participate in the rearing of his children.** A child's corresponding right to protection **from interference in the relationship derives from the psychic importance to him of being raised by a loving, responsible, reliable adult." Franz v. U.S., 707 F 2d 582, 595^Q599; US Ct App (1983).**

"A parent's right to the custody of his **or her children is an element of "liberty" guaranteed by the 5th Amendment _and the 14th Amendment_ of the United States Constitution."**

Matter of Gentry, 369 NW 2d 889, MI App Div (1983).

There is a family right to privacy, which the state cannot invade or it becomes actionable for civil rights damages." Griswold v. Connecticut, 381 US 479, (1965).

"One of the most precious rights possessed by parents is the right to raise their children free of government interference. That right, "more precious than mere property rights," is a liberty interest, protected by the substantive and procedural Due Process Clauses of the Fourteenth Amendment." Stanley v. Illinois, 405 U.S. 645, 92 S.Ct. 1208, 31 L.Ed.2d 551 (1972

The natural parents are entitled to the custody of their minor children, except when they are unsuitable persons to be entrusted with their care, control, and education, or when some exceptional circumstances appear which render such custody inimical to the best interests of the child.

While **_the right of a parent_** to the custody of its infant child is therefore, in a sense, contingent, the right can never be lost or taken away so long as the parent properly nurtures, maintains, **and cares for the child."** Wilson v. Mitchell, 111 P. 21, 25-26, 48 Colo. 454 (Colo. 1910)

For two little girls ...to be taken... and an agency worker who knew the truth. But, would rather hinder, when knowingly to disclose, is shocking the conscience, of many worldwide.

Sadly...

Such parent, the author, for almost a decade was deprived the fundamental right to continue to raise, nuture her own children, denied such parental rights, even though it was clear, she was more than a fit, educated astute loving good parent to her daughter's, and had no history whatsoever of drug-addiction, alcoholism, et.al, as the APPEAL (NJ highest court)made reference to how such action(s)by the DIVISION(DCPP,DCF)had affected her parental rights. CPS employee still ignored such decision for years, in violation of such parent's right to her own girls.

-Chapter V-
Reasonable Effort By:
(DCPP,DCF,DHS,DYFS)

Such reasonable effort by a state employee @ CPS, was not made.

Parent has a right to procure custody-return of their NJ Child"if"reasonable effort was applied, by DYFS. The right to one's child shall occur when the "Division"has made such available, reasonable efforts to provide __*services*__ to help the parent,*correct* the circumstances *__which led__* to the child's placement **outside the home**.

The parental rights of author, were not suppose to be severed, as experts cite, basically that is just what happened, as her right to her girls were not for days,weeks,months but inexcusably for years non-existent, in violation of her most basic rights.

Unilaterally for years, attorney cite for years, by the name of Mr.J.D.Gordon of Bergen County argued in state court 07-2010 that DCPP have basically terminated the mother constitutional right and legal right to her own girls while breaking law(s)in the process. The girls suffered immensely"entire time 03-2012.

Case law support wholly, the parent rights in NJ cannot just simply extinguish an unsuccessful parent-child relationship without making first, provision for a more promising relationship in the child's future." This is done through TITLE 9's mandate of DYFS "services/case plan."The initial case plan involving DYFS and the mom (that will help through discovery commencing October 2013 is the initial plan that clearly had express, "Goal *is to return* children to the home, of the mother." This was *never* mention again, for several years by DYFS, who feign as if it "did not exist."But it did and ergo will support author family significant lawsuit portion of the claims filed against D.Y.F.S.

Didn't matter however to all defendants(see complaint)of their names/positions et;al.,

Who did indeed, severe parent-child relationship,in violation of one's constitutional right.

This is a composite picture of what is by law, under TITLE 9-30 action involving NJ DYFS, necessary to advance the best interests of the children, case law support for decades.

However the "best"interest involving mom, as shared in the girls' lawsuit, and their mom was lost for a total shocking, of almost eight years.

For reasons, articulated in the federal action involving mom and daughter's,

we believe and have interview hundreds of attorneys, no embellishment, but over 100 lawyers, (who at first) refuse to represent author, but yet agreed, such lawsuit is clear.

Agreeing:

Mom's family civil rights lawsuit claim(s)for well-deserved damages is there, and **are ripe** for a jury damages trial if not (reasonably settled) adding that the family have argued at the *pro-se* level relevant the "Constitutional Fundamental Right" of a child and or of the actual loving parent to be with child and the

A CONSTITUTIONAL RIGHT TO GO HOME ...

child to **not** be ignored when one's constitutional right is clearly supported by dozens of case law here and nationwide. Such lawsuit for money damages has been filed pro-se.

The DYFS attempted in 2012,throughout 2013,2014,2015,2016, to have it dismiss but <u>failed</u>, relating to the author's multi-million $$$ suit,for CIVIL RIGHT DAMAGES ...

D.Y.F.S. newly assigned lawyer attempted to argue,

" well, she filed before." This was his thinly-weak argument for some time, and did not defend ANY of the serious allegation(s) (quoting federal magistrate) against his employees on the hook for damages involving such children and the innocent good parent.

However, Judge shut this argument down by adaging,

"DEFENDANTS"are only still focusing on the "removal"of her daughter,as this is the claim she,the mom filed 08. Such lawsuit for damages was premature.(meaning author filed 1st one too soon.) Judge Linares understood through a cogent argument presented by the mother, who, at such time, was suing for not the wrongful removal, as yes this was the claim and it was untimely hence, premise on the S.O.L.(statute of limitations expiring) her lawsuit was not decided on the actual merit, but dismissed premise on the SOL.

Ergo, the state has lost a significant argument, against a Pro-se self file litigant.

Judge agree with plaintiff,"her claim(s) **_are not_** for the wrongful removal."

If an attorney take her lawsuit and daughter, he will be able to properly enumerate this for the court, in a much better position that author had attempted, but for now has work brilliantly for a pro-se litigant without a lawyer, who was able to keep her $50 million lawsuit moving forward, in a way literally pro-se litigants are **_not able_** and in such manner all "lawyers" who agreed she has a significant set of claim(s)for damages, did not "care" about her rights enough or the girls rights, violation, to represent the family.

 Pragmatically, the lawsuit (if dyfs)was paying attention will understand this is not the same claim, that is precluded if it was the 'identical-same claim' from the one filed in 08. I personally believe CPS just simply do not see what **is clear** and has attempted

in this lawsuit to"do what they have done for almost eight years"in state. But this is not going to happen in U.S.District Federal Court,premise on the fact such federal judge, **is** paying attention and is not acting bias as the family court judges have.

A CONSTITUTIONAL RIGHT TO GO HOME ...

This is a blessing for such author and her girls to receive finally JUSTICE through the money damages, and to hear,

"Your rights indeed were violated as an American citizen who were entitled by law to be reunited as a family under one roof, and that such violation by a caseworker/state employee was not at any time reasonable.

The lawsuit ergo,is able to move forward. Media has aired such relevant story.

The search for the "right lawyer" to take over, as we now lead into such Discovery (after 10 years of such pain indescribable) involving mom/the girls,finally get to see ALL of the available discovery, things mom did not know.(But the caseworker knew.)

After so long we are bless to have discovery and interrogatories et;al against a agency,and its workers, supervisory, managerial who assume they will get away with it.

-Bonus Chapter-

<u>CASE LAW...</u>

Author,the plaintiff, in her first oppositional(not the 2nd

Amended-Complaint)was able to present multiple case law to
support as to"why"her lawsuit along with child should stand,
and not be tossed out premise on Res Judicata/Collateral
Estoppel.(State lost another legal argument against mom, who
stood her ground firm.) <u>She, all on her own has</u>
<u>proven just that.</u>

Res Judicata, Collateral Estoppel did <u>not</u> exist and
judge agreed, not once but repeatedly.

Case law support/and or make reference(s)to what
the state has lost when attempting to have this
much-warranted lawsuit for money damages
dismissed. To us, here at our effective **inspiring**
network, the hardest part,in our consensus, as
expert(s) agree,along with an astute attorney who
always give us free input here at our pro-se effective
motivational learning women's ctr, as Paul,an
attorney in tort/civil rights law has cited that:

> ➤ The first hurdle is usually the hardest,"getting past the actual immunities **MOTION TO DISMISS**" and we have done just that our family.

Underscore(when attorney reviewed the entire case-file)and notes that as case law fully support:

Children, deeply need an association with a nurturing adult.

Because permanence in family court cases,

that involve DYFS(DCPP) DCF,that such has been seen as an important aspect of nurturing, it must be evaluated carefully by the court with factual information that is relevant involving the parent in question,the children home-life, not to be kept from a loving parent, whose **always** worked and raise both girls, never smoke, nor ever drink, a young homeowner who purchase home on her own,(just prior) to all of this expensive litigation, and the state's unwarranted premise on D.Y.F.S. who by their own admission and or withheld evidence supporting fact that per state employee willfully and or by such

A CONSTITUTIONAL RIGHT TO GO HOME ...

reckless intentional disregard elect to hinder, rather than to disclose, had for some time,

withheld evidence of a loving suburban parent innocence, withholding fact(s) in a report, internal CPS report that:

- ➢ Mom was a lovely well-spoken young lady.
- ➢ Mom was innocent.
- ➢ False allegation (At the time by a jealous troubled father's family/his mom was clearly making such falsity without evidence to support such clear falsehood) and how there was no substantiation of abuse and or neglect.

- ➢ Such bombshell **FACT** was documented, in a four page report, memorialized by the actual caseworker <u>for the state agency!</u>

This is unlawful.

 No lawyer nor expert has disagreed once such "box of evidence withheld has surfaced.

CHAPTER VI-

"A **Special Relationship** with a state employee entitle such plaintiff to civil right damages along with such **FORESEEABLE** danger..."

D.A.G. for state defendant(s)attempted to cite how there was absolutely "no special relation" insofar as child plaintiff,and her or her mother.

Clearly ... this is false...

Case law is not in any way unclear.

The foreseeable danger, was clearly at the time known to at least multi-caseworkers for Union County DYFS(DCPP) and also a CPS supervisor during the time both were assigned to the case involving the author girls.

 A total lack of supervision constitutes, along with the depraved, deliberate indifference to the plaintiff (author) and her girls **for almost eight years,** to suffer untold damages, while defendant(s)DCPP DCF had knowingly continued her ruse, by stating the girls were fine,**not at any risk,** and how the step-mom is such a wonderful person, as the father, are both taking "good care of the girls."

All was false, later to be proven by such gruesome withheld file.

Such lack of supervision, while under state care, constitute a lack of ordinary care, involving JS and or her supervisor MD, CN, and other defendants, in which those who were at the time responsible for the girls well-being."

A supervisor herein M.D., as case law wholly support, can be held vicariously liable for injuries proximately caused, by such negligence. Such lies, knowingly false information, has deprive mom of her Due-Process for almost eight years, to a fair hearing, where all *TRUTHFUL* information, if submitted to the court,

for the judge to adjudicate, a reasonable juror can conclude, the girls would have been either:

a.) return home, with all truthful information supplied to the court since 2004 throughout 2010 and or would have most likely as a reasonable jury can conclude.

b.) **Resulted** in a fair-hearing under the Due Process Clause of our fourteenth amendment, for mother to reclaim her girls, instead of hearings where the judge had relied on all false information disseminated by these defendants for almost eight years

i.e,

 a relevant "report for example" where the judge specifically ask, on September **2008** and or 2009, how are her girls doing.

Two or more of the actual defendant's in the author meritorious civil rights lawsuit had earlier agreed how the girls were with dad and doing just **fine,** and yet entire time the caseworker shockingly and knowingly,

hid_the truth that 1 of the girls were prior homeless in early part of 2008,as verified by mother custody lawyer JONATHAN D. GORDON and then later verified by the withheld reports the gruesome truth.

Additionally,

The author daughter's were now getting older and able to simply tell what has happened. The older daughter several times, was able to tell the police what happened during her horrific time under state CPS (dcpp)supervision for years,as her sister.

States may not permit recovery of presumed or punitive damages, at least when liability is not based on a showing of **knowledge of falsity or**

reckless disregard, **is that "punitive** damages
**are permitted when such `actual malice' is
shown."** *Embrey v. Holly,* 293 Md. 128, 442 A.2d
966, **972 n. 14 (1982); See** *also Davis v.
Schuchat* 510 F.2d 731, **737 (D.C. Cir.1975)**

Nothing in the author state, relating to such tort
claim(s)act,as enumerated, clearly established, in
this act shall exonerate a public employee from
liability *if* it is established that his conduct was
outside the scope of his employment, or **constituted
a crime, actual fraud**, actual **malice** or willfull
misconduct." See also, Burke v. Deiner supra, at
472 (where aggravating circumstances exist, the
plaintiff's symptoms can be found to be permanent
"even without residual physical injury.) See, Collins
v. Union County, 150N.J. 407 (1997)

Such circumstances, under which state public
employees *(DYFS)* *are not* immuned from
liability,and are not exonerated from such liability.

1. *Outrageous Conduct*

N.J.S.A. **59:3-14 provides that: Nothing in this act shall
exonerate a public employee from liability if it is
established that his conduct was outside the scope of his
employment or constituted a crime, actual fraud, actual
malice or willful misconduct.**

It is the intent of this provision that a public employee guilty of <u>outrageous conduct cannot</u> avail himself of the limitations as to liability and damages contained in such Tort Claims Act.

In the author's lawsuit supporting such claim for damages, the caseworker J.S.,et.al., clearly knew as her supervisor MD.,knew of severe injuries to the child yet elect to hinder rather than to disclose, knowing as already stated, it would have lead to the girls returning to their mother and a fair hearing as required, when a child under state supervision has been harmed while under state supervision with an open court case,FN matter in New Jersey.

This 1972 Task Force Commentary contained in <u>N.J.S.A.</u> 59:3-14 represents a clear + unambiguous expression of legislative intent that a public employee should be deprived of any benefits such as TCA limitations on liability and damages for their "outrageous" conduct.

Courts have found such "outrageous" conduct, ***thereby removing*** the TCA defenses from public employees, in a multitude of circumstances, including claims for

(1) <u>assault and battery</u>, <u>Velez</u>, <u>supra</u>;

A CONSTITUTIONAL RIGHT TO GO HOME ...

(2) malicious prosecution, <u>James v. Price</u>, 602 <u>F. Supp.</u> 843 (D. N. J. 1985)

(3) knowing violation of drug prescription regulations, <u>Taglieri v. Moss</u>, 367 <u>N.J. Super.</u> 184 (App. Div. 2004)

(4) <u>false arrest</u>, <u>DelaCruz v. Borough of Hillsdale</u>, 365 <u>N.J. Super.</u> 127 (App. Div. 2004);

(5) torts based on reckless conduct, <u>Jobes v. Evangelista</u>, 2004 <u>WL</u> 1170507 (App. Div. 2004) and <u>Alston v. City of Camden</u>, 168 <u>N.J.</u>170 (2001)

"The question of whether Defendants' actions constituted "outrageous" conduct is a question for the jury.

<u>**See Marley v. Borough of Palmyra**</u>, 193 <u>N.J. Super.</u> 271, 295 (App. Div. 2000)(holding that the issue of whether the public employee defendants' conduct was outside the scope of the employment.

CHAPTER VII-

<u>Willful Misconduct ...</u>

<u>N.J.S.A.</u> 59:3-14 provides:

a. <u>Nothing</u> in this act shall exonerate a public employee from liability if it is established that his conduct was outside the scope of his employment or constituted a crime, actual fraud, actual malice or <u>**willful misconduct**</u>.

b. <u>Nothing</u> in this act shall exonerate a public <u>employee from the full measure of recovery</u> applicable to a person in the private sector if it is established that his conduct <u>was outside the scope</u> of his employment or constituted a crime, actual fraud, actual malice or <u>willful misconduct</u>.

Chapter VIII

<u>Reckless Conduct</u>

"<u>Reckless conduct</u>" also deprives Defendants of any protections under the TCA specifically its verbal threshold. In <u>Dunlea v. Township of Belleville</u>, 349 <u>N.J. Super.</u> 506, 512, 513 (App. Div. 2002), the Court held that, in order ***<u>to defeat</u>*** a claim of good faith immunity, ***<u>it is sufficient</u>*** that the plaintiff shows the defendant acted <u>recklessly</u>.   (Emphasis added).

 In addition, in <u>Alston v. City of Camden</u>, 168 <u>N.J.</u> 170, 185 (2001) **the Supreme Court** of New Jersey articulated that ***"willful misconduct"*** <u>is the equivalent of reckless disregard for safety</u>, ***which is more*** than an absence of good faith."
(Emphasis added).

According to <u>Prosser & Keeton on the Law of Torts</u>:

"Reckless conduct" is defined as follows:

A CONSTITUTIONAL RIGHT TO GO HOME …

"An actor acts recklessly ***when he or she intentionally*** commits an act of an unreasonable character in ***disregard of a known or obvious risk*** that was so great as to make it ***highly probable*** that harm would follow,

 and which thus is usually accompanied by a ***conscious indifference*** to the consequences."

Now…
In the author's civil rights lawsuit for civil damage(s) et.al.,

The D.A.G. representing such liable worker's cite how there was simply no fact(s)exerted by mom and daughter that would support a claim, and malice, reckless do not apply. That there isn't any malice, wrongdoing, and or any violation. NONE.

Experts say to the owner or T.A.N. and Women4Justice:

" THIS CASE CRIES OUT FOR A JURY WHO WILL AGREE THERE IS AN OBSCENE AMOUNT OF SUCH WILLFUL CONDUCT, UNBECOMING TO A STATE EMPLOYEE, ALONG WITH SUCH RECKLESSNESS THROUGHOUT ALMOST EIGHT YEARS OF DEALING WITH SUCH AGENCY, STATE EMPLOYEES @ CPS."

Experts hearing and or reading such always chuckle at such weak, thinly-argument presented by a state agency that the worker's did nothing wrong/have not engage in any malice and or did not misrepresent the actual over facts.

A CONSTITUTIONAL RIGHT TO GO HOME ...

Such agency, as experts agree, and lawyers who are watching and following such publicized lawsuit, all unanimously agree, Division (DCPP,DYFS,CPS) are for so many years known to:

- ➤ <u>Violate.</u>
- ➤ <u>Demonstrate</u> *sloppy incompetence from what they refer to as "overworked employees for such state agency.*
- ➤ <u>Known</u> to cause harm to so many children under state supervision.

Author is told by so many lawyers, "no reasonable minded jury shall disagree <u>and will</u> do what is <u>right.</u>"

Another example/fact involving caseworker in such publicized lawsuit:

Caseworkers are suppose to adhere to such policy and report to the agency(I.A.I.U.) if abuse of child under state DCF supervision is known.

This did not happen in the author's prior family court case, in violation of such rights of the child and mother.

J.S. and or C.N., MD., **never bothered to report such factual.**

Never reported to the I.A.I.U.(agency to investigate foster abuse injuries et.al., since it would have come out to mom/her lawyer et.al., along with the judge the child was "not thriving and not doing well at the home of the troubled father and step-mom.

This is easily able to be proven as lawyers and experts all agree."

Such DCPP defendants not at any time for years advise the judge adjudicating that:

a. Child was in the hospital.

b. Child was bounced from foster stranger home, to another home, repeatedly.

c. Child was missing. (A.P.B.) was put out to locate/attempt to find juvenile-child.

d. Child was assaulted(brutally)multi-times while under state supervision.

e. Child was also homeless for some time.

f. Child was no longer allowed back in the house owned by step-mom.

g. Child was force-separated from her sister.

h. Child was **not** doing "fine at all.

i. Child was not "thriving whatsoever as a caseworker falsely reported multi-times.

Caseworker J.S., the defendant as a favor to J.M. her close personal friend, or family relative, unfairly distracted, and with the agency its focus from the central question of such, insofar as:

When working outside the scope of defendant employment, as clearly J.S. the assigned caseworker, failed to properly exercise her duties, as officials in such self-governing democracy, that she stated false-facts et.al., mislead the court, in which she knew,

and or reasonably should have known to be **FALSE.**

CHAPTER XI

-SUMMARY JUDGEMENT-

On summary judgment, a plaintiff must produce evidence "sufficient" to establish the existence of an element essential to that party's case, and on which that party will bear the burden of proof at trial." <u>Celotex Corp. v. Catrett</u>, <u>477 U.S. 317, 322-23</u> (1986).

Mere allegations are **not** enough to survive summary judgment. <u>S.E.C. v. J.W. Barclay Co.</u>, <u>442 F.3d 834, 840</u> (3d Cir. 2006) (<u>quoting</u> Fed.R.Civ.P. 56(e).

" In the author's lawsuit, she has submitted more than <u>enough </u>facts, shocking the conscience of seasoned detectives, to lawyers coast-to-coast, of such relevance, as already shared in such volume of books now being released, and verified in the news."

Author has provided **substantial** evidence and fact(s)that rise above a mere "allegation, as her daughter."

Experts cite that it is more than enough of what is needed,required in the U.S.District Federal Court, and a jury shall be able to conclude what the family has waited on for over 10 to 13 years and growing . . .

Such evidence, as required in these type of cases for damages, per constitutional/civil right violations, would permit, at each turn, a jury to conclude that something horrific involving a state employee had taken place, **against mom and her daughter's, at no fault of their own.**

There are no bald assertions, false fact(s) presented by author, and daughter's.

Hence, sufficient facts, and evidence, shall be, and are enough to defeat summary judgement, involving child protection agency state employees. Such evidence, is enough to support a conclusion(as required) to support such conclusion that a **CONSTITUTIONAL** right, of **mom/and or such children were violated by C.P.S. employee, and or employees.**

Summary Judgement is where you're wanting to be, when suing a state employee pursuant to damages, U.S.C.A.Title 42 Section 83.

This is when you're able everyone to learn if presented strongly,accurately,clear and concise, with such overall fact(s) and supportive case law, you're able to God-willing win the right to have a jury trial assess your claim(s)per cause of action for your damages, you're seeking.

Many, when suing a state employee might not reach such relevant point of litigation(when suing for monetary damages) but author has reached such relevant point as media publicly validate.

We hope you are going to as well everyone ...

Keep in mind that, at summary judgement, such movant, for which is the actual defendant(CPS and or a **state** employee et.al,)that such **DEFT**, known as the "movant" actually has the burden to prove the absence of a genuine issue of material fact, that such genuinely-disputed material fact regarding the claims at issue, simply does not exist. The actual non-moving party(<u>YOU</u>) the plaintiff, must in response, must "go beyond the pleadings and by her own affidavits, or by the depositions, answers to interrogatories, and admissions on file, designate **specific facts** showing **that there is a genuine issue for trial."**

(THIS IS CRUCIAL) so #learn #studyhard when suing such state employee for damages, like our owner has done correctly/timely.

> **State agency lawyer shall always exert the fact that, "there is just no genuine issue of such fact, to be presented to a jury for damages, and the suit should be dismissed, in its entirety, based on what is known as "matter of law."**

"**_A dispute_** about a material fact is genuine if the evidence **_is sufficient_** to permit a reasonable jury to return a verdict for the non-moving party." Lamont v. New Jersey, 637 F.3d 177, 181 (3d Cir. 2011) (internal citation and quotation omitted)

I.E.(in example)as cited in all other book releases **under** WOMEN 4 JUSTICE PUBLISHING N.Y.C., et.al,

1.)Child **is** removed.

2.Child was **not** injured...Not at the level **needed** to remove a child/keep a child from ever going home.

3.) There was no imminent danger/exigent circumstance relating to removing a child without the necessary court order, or a warrant that would have legally allowed such agency worker to take child into state custody,to be lawfully seized.

3.)Caseworker/state employee cites in a report child is "alert/happy/healthy/no serious injuries and no neglect.

4.)Child is doing fine/was not injured at all and was able to return home.

5.)Social worker assigned/DCPP can't substantiate abuse/neglect/injuries consistent with such abuse by a parent et.al., caretaker.

6.)Social worker memorialize in a report,

"Agency CPS has no legal right, nor legal basis, nor any authorization to keep child away from returning home.

Yet...

Such agency says later, when sued that:

A. We did nothing wrong, federal court.
B. Caseworker was only doing what was at the time, on the day in question required.
C. Lawsuit can't move forward to trial since after all the caseworker was only acting in "Good faith, on day in question."

All experts coast to coast from:

 NJ, DELAWARE tri-state

to Maryland, PA., to California, Arizona, all agree.

This is a clear GENUINE ISSUE OF MATERIAL FACT, that can ONLY BE DECIDED by a jury of one's peers involving author and her daughter.

Another example for our many supporters and viewer's.

➢ Caseworker issue a report citing how the reason the child did not see mom is simply premised on "1" non-qualified therapist citing, "It will harm/damage child et.al.,

HOWEVER ...

➢ Another therapist,actually a PH.D.level psychologist, who met the girls, unlike the non-qualified therapist, has cited, while also meeting mom, wrote in her report, actually several, "child would benefit by seeing mom, being with mom, and even a "trial period at home again with mom, as this was clear and known at the time to cps agency(dcpp) who **IGNORED** it all.

Such issue is relevant.

Such issue is a material-fact, as lawyers agree.

Such issue @ summary judgement is most relevant.

Another example with a state worker involving such "Genuine issue of material fact, taking right from the winning suit of the author's out of 3rd district and other suits analogous coast to coast:

>Caseworker cites, "Child was removed premise on serious injuries/bruising, in other words ***imminent danger."***

HOWEVER:

wholly supporting a 4th amendment claim, for civil right damages:

Child was, on the day in question:

- A.) <u>HEALTHY</u>
- B.) <u>HAPPY</u>
- **C.)ALERT**
- D.) <u>NOT INJURED</u>
- E.) <u>NO MEDICAL</u> ATTENTION NEEDED(police cite such truthfulness verbatim)
- F.) No need to even go talk to mom since there is no abuse/neglect/no injuries for which is consistent on the day in question that would rise to the level of abuse or neglect. Experts agree, that the child would have not been unconstitutionally detained/seized (in violation of her 4th amendment,if state employee adhere to such policies, protocol,guidelines,when the girls were only 10/7 years old, hence a jury shall be able to easily conclude that, there was no:

A CONSTITUTIONAL RIGHT TO GO HOME ...

1. Imminent DANGER.
2. No need to keep the girls away from mom.
3. No need to bar children of such good health on day in question from going home.
4. The state worker also was required by law to procure the actual warrant to remove the girls, and or a judicial court order authorization PRIOR to seizure of the girls. Yet took 14 days or so to procure such court order, proving that there was absolutely:

   A.) No imminent danger to either little girl.
   B.) The girls were just fine.
   C.) No government agency interference by CPS employees were warranted on such date.

ALL are GENUINE ISSUES OF SUCH FACT THAT A JURY SHALL BE ABLE TO CONCLUDE, and return a verdict of damages, in favor of such plaintiff's.

CHAPTER X-

-ELEVENTH AMENDMENT-

- SOVEREIGN IMMUNITY-

Eleventh Amendment Immunity the Eleventh Amendment states:

The Judicial power of the United States shall not be construed to extend to any suit in law or equity, commenced or prosecuted against one of the United States by Citizens of another State, or by Citizens or Subjects of any Foreign State. U.S. Const. amend. XI. Case 3:14-cv-04429-MLC-DEA Document 15 Filed 04/01/16 Page 5 of 16

A federal district court may bar a suit under the Eleventh Amendment even when "a state is not named a party to the action, as long as the state is the real party in interest."

A CONSTITUTIONAL RIGHT TO GO HOME ...

Fitchik v. N.J. Transit Rail Operations, Inc., 873 F.2d 655, 659 (3d Cir. 1989) (en banc).

Thus, Eleventh Amendment immunity extends to state departments and agencies that are "arms of the state."

Bowers v. Nat'l Collegiate Athletic Ass'n, 475 F.3d 524, 545 (3d Cir. 2007) (internal citation omitted).

In a nutshell everyone ...

Bringing a lawsuit with a lawyer/and or pro-se(self file) against state employees, pertaining to such 11th amendment shall be barred, if sued in a state employee INDIVIDUAL CAPACITY,so learn and study hard on such,

as the author has done for over 13 years and growing.

Such lawsuit of a state employee in her/his individual capacity is not barred as case law wholly support by our 11th amendment.

Remember:

Eleventh Amendment immunity does <u>not</u> apply, in their individual capacities.

Hafer v. Melo, 502 U.S. 21, 31 (1991).

CHAPTER 11

<u>A STATE EMPLOYEE SHALL INVOKE WHAT IS KNOWN AS "QUALIFIED IMMUNITY FROM SUIT."</u>

"The doctrine of qualified immunity protects government officials from liability from paying out civil damages insofar as their conduct does **<u>not</u>** violate clearly established statutory or constitutional rights of which a ***<u>reasonable</u>*** person would have known." Pearson v.

Callahan, 555 U.S. 223, 231 (2009)

Qualified immunity grants immunity from suit, and applies even when a government official committed an error based upon "a mistake of law, a mistake of fact, or a mistake based on mixed questions of law and fact."

A federal district court, in order to determine whether qualified immunity applies, must decide whether:

(1) "the facts ... alleged ... or shown ... make out a violation of a constitutional right"; and

(2) "the right at issue was clearly established at the time of defendant's alleged misconduct."

Qualified immunity is an affirmative defense. Halsey v. Pfeiffer, 750 F.3d 273,

288 (3d Cir. 2014).

Accordingly, a defendant bears the burden of establishing ==entitlement to a qualified immunity== *defense on a motion for summary judgment.*

With respect to the Fourth Amendment,

a police officer **"who reasonably but mistakenly** concludes that the police officer's conduct comports with the requirements of the Fourth Amendment is entitled to immunity." Palma v. Atl. Cty., 53 F.Supp.2d 743, 769 (D.N.J. 1999).

Courts must analyze the "totality of the circumstances" and adopt a "common sense" approach to the issue of probable cause. United States v. Glasser, 750 F.2d 1197, 1205 (3d Cir. 1984).

In the author's publicized, most warranted civil rights violation suit,

the child's fourth amendment claim for damages, all experts coast-to-coast agree is not in any way unclear.

The author girls, had a *legal right* to return home. The author daughter's were unlawfully seized. The 4th amendment was <u>clearly established</u> at the time of said violation.

A jury, based on case law shall reach such actual conclusion, that the state have violated the family rights involving one's 4th amendment, and **no QUALIFIED IMMUNITY** shall protect such agency worker who:

1. **Acted with clear malice since day one.**

2. **From** the outset hid such truthful fact shared in such book(s) moreover the fact the **caseworker was not** able to substantiate, yet kept 2 little once happy girls from a doting astute, loving parent, the mother, and barred the girls from going home at only 10 and seven years old for almost eight years.

3. **Knowingly** did so, by hindering such truthful four page multi-report later discovered and support 100% the 4th amendment claim along with other claims consistent with our well-established **Fourteenth Amendment et.al.,**

Such **end goal** *of the defendant's in this warranted lawsuit for multi-civil rights violation(s) were to simply by all means,*

➢ **Disrupt** the loving mom/daughter relation.

➢ To purposeful and unlawfully alienate the mother and her little girls.

➢ To **unlawfully** unconstitutionally and to completely **remove her from her children's lives,** as she is a roadblock to placing the girls with an **emotionally-unstable PGM(paternal grandmother)**and troublesome son/new wife of the **troubled son, both with drug histories and or alcohol addiction(s)**but since 1 of the DCPP defendant's were a close friend, with such personal ties to the step-mother, this was the state employee agenda, as easily proven as experts all agree, in such **meritorious lawsuit.**

In summary...

The Juvenile/Family Court involving **DCPP(DYFS,DCF, CPS)** are clearly

Ill-disposed when it come to a good loving American parent fighting for what is right, if falsely accused that is, unless you're armed with:

1. Knowledge of the law.

2. Astute enough to fight and fight hard,never giving up.

3. Prudent insofar as what to do when you're confronted by a state agency worker and a false allegation et.al.

Such agency/and or the family court can be inimical,

 but you are able to win everyone.

Author is living proof of such as her loving family.

The best interest of the children should be of paramount importance...But yet, such "best"interest continue to fall to the waist side.

Our courts, from New Jersey,Delaware to California, Arizona,North Carolina, Florida and nationally, have **consistently** *for some time now, recognize* that a parent-child relationship has constitutional and fundamental significance and can't simply be violated **without** proof of parental unfitness/serious injuries to a child, imminent danger et.al., hence, such lawsuit filed timely by deadline pro-se by the author, is not in any way unclear.

When a little girl or boy goes off on a weekend visit, they are expecting to arrive at home during the finality of such visitation with the other parent.

I am still, as the author haunted by what the girls, my daughter's were thinking knowing I was not at the time going to be able to bring them to the home we shared for the first 10 and seven years of their very young lives, and I vowed to fight as hard as I can to ensure, this never happen again to another family, nationwide ...

 The pain never shall fully leave ever...

Until ...FINAL JUSTICE is handed down soon enough, God willing by such courts of our land.'

The U.S.DISTRICT FEDERAL COURT...

Ext. 920

We thank you for reading another segment in our long-anticipated book series, and ask that you keep the family in your prayers, and know that our WOMEN 4 JUSTICE PUBLISHING NYC AND TAN CIVIL RIGHTS REDRESS et.al, are here for you, til' God calls us home, simply because, we have been where you're at, and we are confident our informative books shall help many as per help/hotline calls coming in for years to our effective network. Even if it helps 1 avoid being violated by such state employee, and or help those realize that they ARE capable, then author's job is done. We thank you, for reading another segment of our docu-series . . .

To Be Continued.

The time is **ALWAYS** right …
To do what is right. . .

M L K JR.

#Our Rights Do Matter

hence, use them or lose them.

#NeverGiveUp

www.ingramcontent.com/pod-product-compliance
Lightning Source LLC
Chambersburg PA
CBHW040845180526
45159CB00001B/324